The Cat Doctor

Written by Susan McCloskey
Photographs by John Paul Endress

CELEBRATION PRESS

Pearson Learning Group

Look at all the cats! They have come to the clinic to see the Cat Doctor. Dr. Givin is a vet. That's short for veterinarian. A veterinarian is a doctor who takes care of animals.

One of the cats is Puff. This is Puff's first visit to Dr. Givin. She has come for a check-up.

Tammy is one of Dr. Givin's helpers. She asks Shane some questions.

"How old is Puff? Is Puff male or female? Does Puff go outside? Are there any other cats in the family? What does Puff eat?" Tammy writes Shane's answers on a chart.

"Come on in!" says Dr. Givin.

Dr. Givin weighs Puff and writes her weight on a chart. Then she checks Puff's eyes. They are clear. Good! She looks at Puff's teeth. They are nice and clean. Good! She looks in Puff's ears. They're clean, too. She listens to Puff's heart. It sounds fine.

Then Dr. Givin checks Puff for fleas with a special comb. She finds a flea. That's not good. Fleas can make a cat sick. Dr. Givin dabs a medicine on Puff's skin to kill the fleas.

Dr. Givin trims Puff's sharp claws. Then she gives Puff her shots. Cats should get shots every year to keep them healthy.

When Puff's check-up is over, she goes back into her cat carrier. She seems to know it is time to go home.

"Thanks, Dr. Givin!" says Shane.

"See you in a year!" says Dr. Givin. Then she gets ready for her next patient.

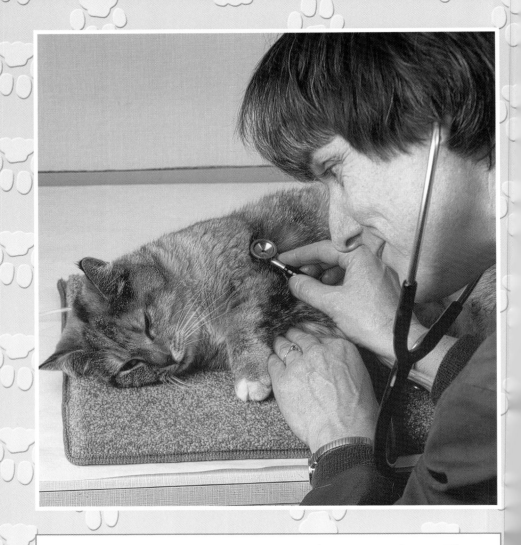

Dr. Givin operated on Misty this morning. The operation will keep Misty from having kittens. This is good. Today, too many kittens and cats need homes. This operation helps prevent that problem. Misty's family is here to take Misty home. With rest she will heal quickly.

Misty has been scratching her ears. So Dr. Givin has taken a sample from Misty's ears and put it under the microscope. She is looking for tiny bugs called ear mites. If she finds any, Dr. Givin will put some medicine into Misty's ears. The medicine will kill the mites.

A cat named Buddy is at the clinic, too. He's having his teeth cleaned. That's Diana's job. She has found a bad tooth. That may be why Buddy has not been eating much. The tooth probably hurts. Diana removes the tooth. When he wakes up, Buddy will feel much better.

Laurie is checking on the other cats at the clinic. She feeds them and cleans their cages. Some are just staying here while their families are away. Dr. Givin will treat the others.

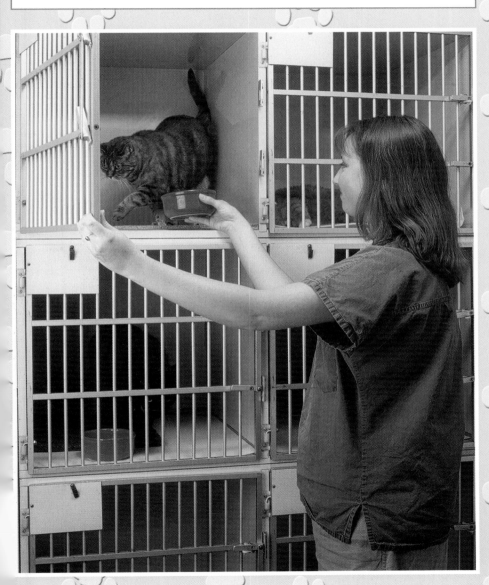

Dr. Givin was seven years old when she decided to become a vet. Is being a vet something you might like to do? Here's what Dr. Givin has to say about becoming a vet.

"Vets have to like animals. But they have to like people, too! That's because vets have to talk with people a lot. They have to ask people questions, listen closely to the answers, and talk about their pets. They also have to help people who are worried and sad because their pets are sick.

"If you want to be a vet, I hope you like school—especially science. It takes a lot of studying to become a vet! Good luck, and study hard!"